War Dogs

AMERICA'S Animal Soldiers

by Meish Goldish

Consultant: Ron Aiello
President of the United States War Dogs Association
Marine Scout Dog Handler

BEARPORT
PUBLISHING

New York, New York

Credits

Cover and Title Page, © Nick Morris/Southcreek Global/ZUMA Press/Newscom and © USAF/Staff Sgt. Suzanne Day/Reuters/Newscom; 4, © Johnny Crawford/Atlanta Journal-Constitution/MCT/Newscom; 5, © Johnny Crawford/Atlanta Journal-Constitution/MCT/Newscom; 6, © The Frank S. Errigo Archive/Getty Images; 7, © AP Photo; 8L, © Bob Owen/San Antonio Express-News/Newscom; 8R, © U.S. Air Force/Senior Airman Christopher Griffin; 9TL, © MaleWitch/Shutterstock; 9TR, © Johan De Meester/ArTerra Picture Library AGE Fotostock; 9BL, © PK-Photos/iStockphoto; 9BR, © P. Wegner/ARCO/AGE Fotostock; 9C, © Animals Animals/SuperStock; 10L, © U.S. Air Force/Senior Airman Staci Miller; 10R, © U.S. Air Force/Master Sgt. Mitch Gettle; 11L, © U.S. Navy/Photographer's Mate Airman Ian W. Anderson; 11R, © U.S. Air Force/Senior Airman Kenny Holston; 12, © U.S. Army/Master Sgt. Lek Mateo; 13, © U.S. Army/Master Sgt. Lek Mateo; 14, © U.S. Air Force/Mr. Kevin Hubbard; 15, © Reuters/K9 Storm Inc./Newscom; 16, © U.S. Air Force/Carl Bergquist; 17, © U.S. Air Force/Tech. Sgt. Johnny L. Saldivar; 18 © Michael Zamora/SHNS/Caller-Times/Newcom; 19, © U.S. Air Force photo by Tech. Sgt. Bennie J. Davis III; 20, © U.S. Air Force/Staff Sgt. Dilia Ayala; 21, © Romeo Gacad/AFP/Getty Images/Newscom; 22TL, © William Munoz; 22TR, © Okapia/Hund/Kramer/Photo Researchers, Inc.; 22BL, © AP Photo/The Lowell Sun/Julia Malakie; 22BR, © Tannen Maury/EPA/Landov.

Publisher: Kenn Goin
Editorial Director: Adam Siegel
Creative Director: Spencer Brinker
Design: Debrah Kaiser
Photo Researcher: Picture Perfect Professionals, LLC

Library of Congress Cataloging-in-Publication Data

Goldish, Meish.
  War dogs / by Meish Goldish ; consultant, Ron Aiello.
      p. cm. — (America's animal soldiers)
  Includes bibliographical references and index.
  ISBN-13: 978-1-61772-452-7 (library binding)
  ISBN-10: 1-61772-452-1 (library binding)
  1. Dogs—War use—United States—Juvenile literature. 2. Rescue dogs—United States—Juvenile literature. 3. Dogs—Training—Juvenile literature. I. Aiello, Ron. II. Title.
  UH100.G65 2012
  355.4'24—dc23
                                2011037639

For more information, write to Bearport Publishing Company, Inc., 45 West 21st Street, Suite 3B, New York, New York 10010. Printed in the United States of America in North Mankato, Minnesota.

10 9 8 7 6 5 4 3 2

CONTENTS

Three Heroes

One night in February 2010, more than 50 American soldiers were asleep inside a **military base** in Afghanistan. Unknown to the soldiers, a **suicide bomber** was quietly approaching the building where the soldiers slept. Wearing 25 pounds (11 kg) of **explosives**, he tried to sneak inside. Luckily, the enemy did not go unnoticed. Three dogs on the base spotted the bomber. First Sasha began to bark loudly. Then Target and Rufus jumped on the enemy and bit him.

Rufus (left) and Target (right)

Unable to enter the building, the bomber set off his explosives by the door. The powerful blast injured five American soldiers—but all of them recovered from their wounds. The three brave dogs were praised as heroes. They had stopped an attack that could have killed many soldiers.

Sergeant Christopher Duke, one of the soldiers saved by the three dogs, was reunited with Rufus back in the United States.

The blast from the bomb wounded Sasha, Target, and Rufus. Unfortunately, Sasha was hurt so badly that she was unable to recover and had to be put to sleep. Target and Rufus survived their injuries.

A Proud Past

Dogs like Sasha, Target, and Rufus have aided the U.S. **military** for more than 150 years. In the **Civil War** (1861–1865) and World War I (1914–1918), some soldiers brought their own dogs with them. Many of the **canines** served merely as **companions**. Others were used to deliver messages on the battlefield or to guard troops.

Like soldiers, war dogs sometimes wear masks to protect them from breathing poisonous gas.

Dogs that serve in the U.S. **Armed Forces** are officially known as military working dogs, or MWDs.

The United States officially began to use war dogs in World War II (1939–1945). At first the animals only **patrolled** American coastlines to warn of possible enemy attacks. Later, war dogs were sent overseas. They guarded soldiers, **weapons**, **vehicles**, and buildings. They also were trained to attack enemy fighters on **command**.

During the Vietnam War (1957–1975), dogs used their sharp senses of smell and hearing to find enemies hiding in the thick jungle.

The Best Breeds

Target, Rufus, and Sasha were **stray dogs** that had wandered onto an American military base and helped the soldiers there. Most U.S. war dogs, however, are **acquired** in a more official way. Before serving in the military, they go through a training program for about 11 weeks at Lackland Air Force Base in San Antonio, Texas.

MWDs being trained at Lackland Air Force Base

Lackland Air Force Base not only trains war dogs, but also breeds puppies for the program.

Military working dogs at Lackland Air Force Base are trained to serve in the U.S. Army, **Navy**, Air Force, and **Marine Corps**.

The dog **breeds** most often trained at Lackland are German shepherds and Belgian Malinois. These breeds usually make the best war dogs. They possess great size, speed, strength, courage, and intelligence. They also smell and hear extremely well. Other breeds that are trained at Lackland include Dutch shepherds, Labrador retrievers, and golden retrievers.

German shepherd

Belgian Malinois

Labrador retriever

Dutch shepherd

Golden retriever

Survival Skills

At Lackland, **handlers** train their MWDs so that they have the special skills they need for the battlefield. For example, the MWDs learn to sniff out bombs hidden in containers or buried in the dirt. The dogs are taught to **alert** their handlers by sitting down when they **detect** a bomb.

A soldier and his dog are learning how to be lowered from a helicopter.

Dogs use their keen sense of smell to recognize the materials that can be used to make a bomb.

Handlers at Lackland also teach their MWDs the same basic **obedience** skills that any dog owners might teach their pets, such as sitting and staying.

While at Lackland, MWDs are also taught to recognize the enemy and to bite and attack on command. They're also trained to attack, without a command, anyone who is harming their handlers. In addition, to help the animals get used to the sounds of gunfire, the handlers fire weapons near their dogs.

Markey, an MWD, practices attacking an enemy.

Master-at-Arms Second Class Donald Reinhart, a handler in the U.S. Navy, fires his gun near his dog, Goof.

A Trusty Team

After completing their training, a war dog and its handler are assigned to a military base. There, the two work as a team. Doran, a German shepherd, and his handler, Staff Sergeant Gregory Long, served together in Iraq in 2005. One of their jobs was to search vehicles on the base for explosives.

Staff Sergeant Long and his dog, Doran, working together

Sergeant Long compared Doran's 42 teeth to bullets. He said that the dog's bite is strong enough to break a person's arm. Once people see Doran's sharp teeth, they think twice about trying to sneak bombs onto the base. Sergeant Long always feels safe with his dog. "He looks out for me, and I look out for him," said Long. "He is a partner that I would trust my life to."

MWDs become very attached to the people that they work with. When a dog needs to change its handler, it can take several weeks for the animal to learn to trust someone new.

Using his sharp sense of smell, Doran can find explosives that his handler cannot see or smell.

Dressed for Success

Handlers do everything possible to keep their canine partners safe on the job. They even provide the animals with special clothing and equipment for the battlefield. For example, the dogs wear bulletproof vests to protect them from enemy fire and boots to protect their paws from hot sand. They also wear "doggles"—dog goggles—which **shield** their eyes in sandstorms.

Haus, an MWD, wears doggles to keep sand out of his eyes, and boots to keep his paws from getting too hot.

MWDs that are working in the desert are given cooling vests to wear. They protect the dogs from temperatures that can get as hot as 135°F (57°C).

When it is dark out, an MWD on patrol may have a night-vision camera attached to its vest. By sending images back to a handler's **monitor**, the camera allows the soldier to see what the dog is seeing. A tiny speaker on the vest lets the handler give the dog instructions as it walks ahead of soldiers. By using the camera, handlers can spot enemies hidden in the dark, even when they are as far away as 1,000 yards (914 m)—the length of ten football fields.

This MWD searches a building in the dark while wearing a bulletproof vest with a camera attached.

A Close Call

Just as handlers protect their dogs, the dogs watch out for their handlers. Staff Sergeant Robert Brown knows that well. He and his dog, Nero, were patrolling a field in Iraq in 2006. Suddenly, the canine detected a bomb. He managed to alert Brown just before an enemy exploded it.

Nero and Staff Sergeant Robert Brown

Although some **shrapnel** from the bomb still struck Sergeant Brown in the head and leg, he recovered from his injuries. The handler praised Nero for saving his life. He believed he might have been killed if Nero hadn't warned him of the danger. "It could have been a lot worse for us," Brown said.

War dogs, such as Chukky (left), save many lives by detecting bombs before they explode.

A bomb-sniffing dog can detect odors up to 100 times better than a human can.

A Painful Loss

Not all war dog stories end happily. In 2010, Private First Class Colton Rusk was shot when his Marine **unit** came under heavy fire in Afghanistan. His dog, Eli, bravely crawled onto his body to protect him. Although Colton died from his wounds, the Marines saw what a loyal canine partner Eli was.

Private First Class Colton Rusk with his dog, Eli

Colton's family suffered a terrible loss. Military officials wanted to help ease their pain. In 2011, they released Eli from the Marines so he could live with the Rusks in Texas. When the dog arrived, Colton's mother said she felt as if part of her 20-year-old son had been returned to her.

Colton's younger brother, Brady, gets a kiss from Eli after the dog returned from Afghanistan and was adopted by Colton's family.

In the past, all retired MWDs had to be put to sleep. It was believed the animals were too **aggressive** and hard to handle to become household pets. In 2000, however, a law was passed that allows people to **adopt** the dogs after they retire.

The Future for War Dogs

Today about 2,700 MWDs serve in the U.S. Armed Forces. The demand for the lifesaving dogs has grown in recent years. Before the **terrorist** attack on the World Trade Center on September 11, 2001, about 200 dogs were trained at Lackland Air Force Base each year. Today, the number is well over 500.

Robby, a Belgian Malinois, and Senior Airman William Bailey serve in Iraq.

In 2011, about 600 MWDs served in Afghanistan and Iraq. More than 2,000 dogs were on other U.S. military bases around the world.

In 2011, a Belgian Malinois named Cairo played an important role in the takedown of the terrorist Osama bin Laden. The MWD assisted U.S. **Navy SEALs** in Pakistan as they approached and entered bin Laden's **compound**. The successful raid was another reminder that war dogs are one of America's best military weapons.

A U.S. soldier in Afghanistan relaxes with his dog, Zzarr.

More About
Dogs

Some dogs serve in the U.S. Armed Forces. However, these smart and loving animals also help people in many other ways. Here are some examples.

Guide dogs are trained to lead people who are blind from place to place.

Sheepdogs **herd** and guard sheep or other farm animals.

Therapy dogs are trained to provide affection and comfort to people in hospitals, retirement homes, and nursing homes.

Search-and-rescue dogs are trained to locate people after a disaster, such as an earthquake, tornado, hurricane, explosion, or terrorist attack.

acquired (uh-KWYE-urd) gotten

adopt (uh-DOPT) take into one's family

aggressive (uh-GRESS-iv) acting in a threatening or fierce way

alert (uh-LURT) give a warning

armed forces (ARMD FORSS-iz) the military groups a country uses to protect itself; in the United States they are the Army, the Navy, the Air Force, the Marines, and the Coast Guard

breeds (BREEDZ) kinds of dogs

canines (KAY-nyenz) members of the dog family, including pet dogs, wolves, foxes, and coyotes

Civil War (SIV-il WOR) the U.S. war between the Southern states and the Northern states, which lasted from 1861 to 1865

command (kuh-MAND) an order given by someone

companions (kuhm-PAN-yuhnz) people or animals that spend time with someone

compound (KOM-pound) a fenced-in area with buildings inside

detect (di-TEKT) to notice or discover something

explosives (ek-SPLOH-sivz) things that can blow up, such as bombs

handlers (HAND-lurz) people who work with and train dogs or other animals

herd (HURD) to make animals or people move together as a group

Marine Corps (muh-REEN KOR) a branch of the U.S. military whose members are trained to fight on land, at sea, and in the air

military (MIL-uh-*ter*-ee) the armed forces of a country

military base (MIL-uh-*ter*-ee BAYSS) a center for military operations; often a place where soldiers live and from which they operate

monitor (MON-i-tur) a device used to watch transmissions

Navy (NAY-vee) a branch of the armed forces that is responsible for military operations on the seas

Navy SEALs (NAY-vee SEELZ) a small group of sailors in the U.S. Navy who are specially trained to fight at sea, in the air, and on land

obedience (oh-BEE-dee-uhnss) the act of doing what one is told to do

patrolled (puh-TROHLD) walked or traveled around an area to protect it

shield (SHEELD) to protect something or someone

shrapnel (SHRAP-nuhl) small pieces of metal scattered by an exploding bomb or other device

stray dogs (STRAY DAWGS) dogs without owners

suicide bomber (SOO-uh-side BOM-ur) a person who carries out an attack by blowing up a bomb attached to his or her body

terrorist (TER-ur-ist) having to do with individuals or groups that use violence and terror to get what they want

unit (YOO-nit) a group of soldiers that are part of a larger group

vehicles (VEE-uh-kuhlz) machines used to carry people or goods from one place to another, such as cars or trucks

weapons (WEP-uhnz) things that can be used in a fight to attack or defend, such as guns or knives

Index

Bibliography

Dowling, Mike. *Sergeant Rex: The Unbreakable Bond Between a Marine and His Military Working Dog.* New York: Atria Books (2011).

Hamer, Blythe. *Dogs at War: True Stories of Canine Courage Under Fire.* London: Carlton (2006).

Rogak, Lisa. *The Dogs of War: The Courage, Love, and Loyalty of Military Working Dogs.* New York: St. Martin's Griffin (2011).

Read More

Apte, Sunita. *Combat-Wounded Dogs (Dog Heroes).* New York: Bearport (2010).

Goldish, Meish. *Bomb-Sniffing Dogs (Dog Heroes).* New York: Bearport (2012).

Grayson, Robert. *Military (Working Animals).* Tarrytown, NY: Marshall Cavendish Benchmark (2011).

Murray, Julie. *Military Animals (Going to Work).* Edina, MN: ABDO (2009).

Ruffin, Frances E. *Military Dogs (Dog Heroes).* New York: Bearport (2007).

Learn More Online

To learn more about war dogs, visit
www.bearportpublishing.com/AmericasAnimalSoldiers

About the Author

Meish Goldish has written more than 200 books for children. His book *Heart-Stopping Roller Coasters* was a Children's Choices Selection in 2011. He lives in Brooklyn, New York.